MY WINGS

Black & White Edition

Just Patty

Written by: Just Patty
Artwork: Patty van Delft

ISBN: 1496019377
ISBN-13: 978-1496019370

Part 1: My Dark Wings

Dedicated to Shane, my brother

Without him, I would never had the courage to write this

or discover the depths of the dark side of my soul

Thank you my dear Shane

I love ya much bro

Part 2: My Light Wings

Dedicated to Danny, my knight

Without him, I would never be able to stay in the light

or enjoy life the way I do now

Thank you, my love

You have my heart forever

PART I

MY DARK WINGS

A bridge to nowhere

Lost
There is no way out of here
I am hanging on strings
While the puppeteer plays his premier

Dark
Underneath sweet raptured light
Will I ever find salvation?
I lost my will to fight

Stuck
Inside an endless circle
I am spiraling down...
Can I stop, am I able?

Haunted
By memories and questions
My mind is playing tricks
And my sight darkens

So, where do I go?
To escape this insanity
I am on a bridge to nowhere
And I am unable to find me...

So, where do I go?
To escape this insanity
I am on a bridge to nowhere
And I am unable to find me...

Save me

I've been to hell and back
Gone through a lot
Always under attack
Happiness still uncaught

I've done bad things
Had to survive
Spreading my dark wings
To stay alive

I've locked myself in
But I can't get out
I wouldn't know where to begin
Suffering from regret and doubt

I'm hanging on the edge of life
Desperate and broken
Nothing but a lowlife
In this world so barren

I'm about to give up the fight
Nothing is worth it anymore
It's a horror story I can't rewrite
Only you can be my savior

My Black Wings

Even now, now my black wings are damaged
They will always be able to carry me
The darkness inside brings the warrior out
And I fight until there's only light to see

Courage is my name
Strong is my heart
Healing shall be my endgame
Maybe I'll break
But I will never fall apart

Even now, now my black wings are bloody
They will never let me fall
My inner angel won't let the darkness get me
And I shall conquer it all

I Still

I still feel you
Your spirit inside my heart
My guardian angel stays with me
We will never be apart

I still see you
Your blue eyes in the sky
I can't let you go
Our love cannot die

I still hear you
Your voice in my head
Telling me to love life
Comforting me when I'm sad

I still search for you
Everywhere I go, no matter what I do
I am looking and I won't stop
Because someday I will find you

I still love you
Words can never explain
How souls can connect
And love can ease the pain

Can I?

Can I just hold you one more time?
Tell you how much I love you
Just one more week...
One more week will do
Can I?

Can I just hug you one more time?
Show you how much I care
Just one more day...
One more day to share
Can I?

Can I just talk to you one more time?
Until the sunset
Just one more hour...
One more hour to never forget
Can I?

Can I just kiss you one more time?
Hold you so very close
Just one more minute...
One more minute without sorrows
Can I?

Can I just look at you one more time?
To make sure that you are alright
Just one more second...
One more second to say goodnight
Oh please, can I?

Can I at least say goodbye?

Black

Black are my wings
Dark as the night
Produce a fake smile
No strength to fight

Black are the days
Lying behind
No golden sunrays
I am staring blind

Black are the thoughts
Wandering through my head
Can't see the difference
Between good and bad

Black is the world
Pitch dark outside
And all is coming for me
No place to hide

Black is all that remains
I am fighting no more
Dark clouds will be my chains
Behind a Black prison door...

Black
is all that remains
I am fighting no more
Dark clouds will be my chains
Behind a Black prison door...

Anger!

Mad
As hell
Trying to conceal my temper
Fighting to contain my actions

Anger
Blood red
Thoughts are running wild
Spinning out of control

Betrayal
So harsh
The untold truth is choking
Feelings are darkening

Furious
Beyond words
Who are you stranger?
A web of lies is strangling my heart

Tears
Tasting bitter
But the fault is my own
For trusting too easily

Get a grip! Let it go...
Hoping love will conquer my rage
Eventually
If the truth has been told and the reason is discovered...

Am I still here?

Am I still here?
Without your arms around me, I can't feel
It's all a fog, I can't see clear
I don't know if I am real

Am I still breathing?
Without your kiss, I am not sure
It's painful, It's aching
I don't know if I can endure

Am I still awake?
Without your voice, I cannot hear
It's too much, I'm going to break
Is it a week? Is it a year?

Am I still around?
Without your eyes, I can't see
I'm lost, I want to be found
I don't even know if I am still me...

The Darkness is consuming me

Can hear it knocking on my door...
I cover my ears and run
Can't take it anymore
I just wish it was done

Can feel it creeping up on me...
I shiver and try to hide
But I know it can see me
It's right by my side

Can smell it's rotten breath...
I pray and close my eyes
Inside, there's only death
I whisper my goodbyes

Can see it closing in...
And I am screaming silently
This fight I cannot win
The Darkness is consuming me

Drowning in my own tears...

Trying to reach the surface
Fighting for air
But I am drowning
Drowning in my own tears

Trying to wake up
Escape the demons
But I am suffocated
Suffocated by my own fears

Trying to get back up
Struggling to stand tall
But I am broken
Broken by all that I lost

Trying to be alright again
Fighting for survival
But I am imprisoned
Imprisoned by my own thoughts

I am...
Drowning
In my
Own
Tears....

Can you see (All these broken parts of me)

You can see my smile
But can you see my tears?
And if you do
Will you protect me against my fears?

You can see my love
But can you see my pain?
And if you do
Will you shelter me against the rain?

You can see what I have
But can you see what I lost?
And if you do
Will you stay at all cost?

You can see my light
But can you see the dark?
And if you do
Will you relight the spark?

You can see my strength
But can you see my despair?
And if you do
Will you be there?

You can see my courage
But can you see what I won't show?
And if you do
Will you be my hero?

All these broken parts of me
You can't see those if you are just passing by
So can you see
More than meets the eye?

All these broken parts of me
You can't see those if you are just passing by
So can you see
More than meets the eye?

Don't you miss me?

Don't you miss me?
Don't you miss me at all?
Do you ever think of me?
Of all the fun we had...
Cheering each other up when we were feeling sad

Don't you miss me?
Don't you miss me at all?
Remember all the secrets we shared?
All the laughter and every tear...
Are those memories you hold dear?

Don't you miss me?
Don't you miss me at all?
Why didn't you kept your promise?
I kept mine...
But don't worry, I will be fine

Don't you miss me?
Don't you miss me at all?
You really hurt me, you know...
And I despise you for that!
Throwing away everything we ever had

Don't you miss me?
Don't you miss me at all?
I hate you for what you did!
Not having the courage to say it to my face...
You are a coward and a disgrace!

Don't you miss me?
Don't you miss me at all?
Do you know what's the worst of it?
I can't forgive you for what you did!
But deep down, where no one can see...
I still love you, as stupid as that may be

Don't you miss me?
Don't you miss me at all?
Because I do
I really miss you...

In too deep

No rest for the wicked
Guess I'm one of them
No one can be trusted
A mind overrun by mayhem

No salvation for the fallen
Guess I lost my wings
This life is a burden
Shutting down my feelings

No hope for the jaded
Guess I've to endure this alone
All my life I have been hunted
I can't make it on my own

No light in the darkness
Guess this is my fate
I'm in too deep, it's hopeless
Maybe...it's just too late

Darkness is taking over...

Despair, Fear and Grief
They all visit tonight
My heart is frozen, my feelings go numb
If I could only see the light...

Anger, Rage and Loss
They are old friends of mine
My eyes go blind, my mind is locked
The edge to madness becomes a very thin line...

Pain, Crazy and Sorrow
Just won't leave me alone
My memories are clear, but my future is clouded
Destination yet unknown...

Doubt, Captivity and Desperation
Have just arrived
My soul is lost, my love has been choked
Don't know if it can be revived...

Loneliness, Hate and Revenge
Have no secrets for me
My hope crumbled, my spirit is breaking
And Darkness sees its opportunity...

Sadness, Agony and Misery
Came out to play
My courage grows dim, my strength is melting
The light inside me fades away...

Closing up

Closed the hatches
No one is allowed to look inside
Not anymore
Not after you died

Locking the door
No one is getting through
Not anymore
Not after you

Throwing up the barricades
No one is coming close, ever
Not anymore
Not leaving my bunker

Defending harder than ever
No breach in my defense
Not anymore
Without my mask, it's too intense

Closing my eyes
So one can see
The broken and tortured soul
Living inside of me

Closing my eyes

So one can see

The broken and tortured soul...

Living inside of me

Don't worry

No, I am not alright
But maybe someday I will be
I will keep fighting!
So, don't you worry about me...

No, I am not fine
But you just wait and see
I will keep trying!
So, don't you worry about me

No, I am not okay
Will I ever be?
I am just so tired
But don't you worry...
Don't you worry about me

Overdose

Cravings, tearing up my mind
Fighting, with all that I am
Searching deep within
For the strength to give a damn

Cravings, bitter and insanely sweet
Destroying what is left of me
Struggling to resist
That godforsaken misery

Cravings, swallowing me whole
Failing...I have to use!
Tumbling down again
Victim of this self-abuse

Cravings, driving me insane
An outbreak of misbehave
My courage fades away
And once again I become a slave

Cravings, taking over everything
Please, free me from this pain!
Poison rushing to my body
And my life becomes in vain...

The Asylum of my own mind

I stray through the dark, twisted hallways
Alone, but careless
No escape out of here
Only devastating emptiness

Ice cold bars blocking my path
There's no way around
The silence is deafening
I can't hear any sound

I turn and roam the other way
The Darkness keeps me company
Thick stone walls
As far as I can see

My feelings bleed away
Slowly counting the days to come
Until there's nothing left
And I become numb

Not even afraid of my demons anymore
I know I will never be free
My fighting spirit is gone
Along with my sanity

Just blindly walking in circles
There is no door to find
I am locked away for good this time
In the Asylum of my own mind...

Hell's Bells

Hell's bells are pounding in my head
Images flashing before my eyes
Messages from my old friend Death
Present at all goodbyes

Panic is building up inside
I have to flee before I go blind
But there's nowhere I can hide
Can't run from my broken mind

Memories scratching on a locked door
I have to fight to keep them out
Don't want to see what I saw before
But the bells are getting so loud....

Searching for the power deep within
Take control, freeze my heart
Can't let those demons win
But secretly I fall apart

I will smile, it's time to lie
Can't be weak, my mask is in place
I don't cry, keep my head up high
For I've yet another goodbye to face...

Come and find me

Missing you is a torture
Gnawing its way into my soul
Without you, my world is bitter
I have to find you

Don't leave me alone
I will be lost without direction
Crawling through a twilight zone
I will find you

Losing you will break me
In a thousand bleeding pieces
Without you, I feel empty
I need to find you

Stumbling through the darkness
Tears are blinding my sight
When I lose my way inside hopelessness
Will you come and find me?

Stumbling through the darkness
Tears are blinding my sight
When I lose my way inside hopelessness
Will you come and find me?

Nightmare

Just the other day
I was thinking of you
Thought you left me for good
Thinking I got through

But then, you came this night
Creeping up on me again
Leaving me, shivering in agony
While laughing like a madman

You make me sick
You make me cry
Haunting me with heartbreaking memories
Let me believe happiness is just a lie

Will I ever get rid of you?
So I finally can be free
Will I recover from your last attack?
So I can finally be just me

Your pure, dark soul
Persistent hunger to break my spirit
The disgusting image you engrave in my mind
Leaving me screaming in my blanket

But I will keep fighting
With everything I possess
And I promise you, my devilish Nightmare
I will get out of your mess...

Pieces

Silently
I stare at the pieces surrounding me
Feeling numb
My eyes turn misty

Reaching out, touching the sharp edges
Feeling pain
Sorrow that last for ages

Defeated, I will hang my head
Feeling discouraged
All my tears are already shed

Don't want to move, just keep still
Feeling hopeless
This can't be happening, this isn't real

Scraping together, every splinter I possess
Feeling sad
Just have to keep going, I guess

Tired, picking up the pieces of my shattered life again
Feeling angry
Someday I will be fine, but until then...
I'll keep picking up the pieces surrounding me

Missing the real you

I am missing you so much
No, that's not true
I miss the person that was you

I need you right now
No, not anymore
I need the one you were before

I want to talk to you
No, that's not right
I want to talk to the person you were at first sight

I miss the fun we have
No, I miss the fun we had
Before everything got really bad

Do you remember that person?
The one who kept my nightmares at bay
Did he really just go away?

I still love you, the one you are for real
The one I met, I really do
But now I'll have to ask...Who are you?

Depression

Behind your smile, I can see your tears
Inside my heart, I can feel your fears
In your eyes, I can see your broken dreams
And I know how desperate it all seems

Behind your strength, I can see your despair
Inside my soul, I feel that it isn't fair
In your voice, I can hear your pain
And I know that you're struggling to stay sane

I need you to know that you matter to me
When I look at you, I believe in what I see
I need you to feel my love for you
Giving up on you is something I will never do

Listen to my words: I care for you
Look into my eyes and you will see it's true
I will fight on your side, I know you want to be free
Please, don't let Depression take you away from me

I am at War!

I am ready, the battle is near
Be strong, be brave
Show them no fear
I am at war

Will you fight along my side?
Stand your ground
Or will you run and hide?
I am at war

I shall fight and never quit
Stab, turn, defend
Taking on every hit
I am at war

They will try to break me
But I'll be fighting back
Until I am where I'm supposed to be
I am at war

No! I am not giving in
I will not surrender
Sure I am going to win
I am at war

I am at war
Fighting my demons
The end of battle is not far
Fighting for my future

So what will it be?
I could use some help...
Will you fight with me?
I am at war!

Shattered trust

Here it comes again
The pain of betrayal
Just the price I have to pay
For being way too loyal

It hits me hard again
The pain of abandonment
Just a follow-up
On being naïve and ignorant

There it is again
The pain of losing faith
Anger grows inside
I am fighting against hate

I fall down again
The pain of shattered trust
Is there no one who's real?
My spirit is being crushed

Can't do this again
Too many broken promises
Maybe I will just give up on love
My heart can't handle anymore bruises

I remember...

I remember your smile
How can I ever forget?
Even after all this time...
I remember our friendship without regret

I remember your laugh
Like it was only yesterday
From the day I met you
I knew you couldn't stay

I remember your kindness
Even through all of your pain
You could make everyone feel better
Your inner sun chasing away the rain

I remember your dreams
And how you shared them with me
But now you're in heaven
Looking down on me

I remember you, my friend
Gone way too soon
And I really miss you sometimes
When I gaze at the stars and the moon

I remember...like I always will
No matter what I do
I remember all those things that made you special
And I will forever love you

No Escape

Wandering through the Valley of Emptiness
Haunted by old demons and new
Trying to escape the loneliness
I can't stop thinking of you

Strolling over the Path of a Lost Mind
My love for you is breaking me
Trying to find a way out, I got left behind
I shall never be free

Walking on Memory Lane
Can't seem to get through
My life will just never be the same
Never the same without you

Crawling through the Woods of Vulnerability
The surroundings of a bitter landscape
Because of the emptiness inside me
There is no escape

Revenge

Someday, my time will come
And you shall pay the price
For what you have done
You will see, I am not that nice

Someday I will haunt you
I will promise you that
Now you don't have a clue
But you shall wish we never met

Someday, because I won't forget
And no one will hear you beg for mercy
You ain't seen nothing yet
So listen to this closely

Someday you'll answer for your actions
You just wait and see
And you will know what happens
When you mess with my family

Someday I will find you
I don't care how long it will take
Or what I'll have to do
I never break a promise I make...

Lost...

Lost my mind
Somewhere along the way
Would you be so kind?
And tell me it's going to be okay

Lost my faith
In this damned place
Can you show me something else than hate?
Just a safe breathing space

Lost my direction
Don't know where to go
Can I ask you a question?
How do I get out of the shadow?

Lost my dream
All is at stake
Are you what you seem?
Or just another fake

Lost my soul
Because I gave it away
Could you make me whole?
Just for one day...

Lost my soul
Because I gave it away
Could you make me whole?
Just for one day...

Surviving the Night

Shivering, I listen to the birds
Softly singing their morning song
The night is finally over
A new rising dawn

Gently, small rays of sunlight
Kissing the morning dew
I feel so relieved
Again, I made it through

The upcoming sun chases away
The cold, dark shadows of the night
Breathing a little easier now
I am still alright

The demons of my wicked memory
Will not chase me after sunrise
Slowly and very carefully
I open my eyes

Still shaking of the maddening thoughts
That are lurking inside my head
For now, I am free...
Until the night falls again, a never sleeping threat

Mixed feelings

I want to scream
As loud as I can
Harsh and mean
I hate you!

I want to shout
On the top of my lungs
Giving up, stepping out
How could you?

I want to cry
Until I'm out of breath
Why did you lie?
I despise you!

I want to hold you close to me
Keep you here forever
And I whisper honestly

No matter what, I still love you...

Two Me's

One all crawled up inside
One fighting for my life
The reason I haven't died...

Just keep breathing
Keep my heart pumping
I will be fine

One is crying silently
The other is screaming a battle cry
And they both are me

Just keep breathing
Keep my heart pumping
I will be alright

One is hiding scared
One is standing, fists raised to the sky
So many feelings still unshared

Just keep breathing
Keep my heart pumping
I will stay alive

One is broken and alone
The other numbly pushes through
This battle is my own

Just keep breathing
Keep my heart pumping
I will be good

One worthless, demolished
One proud, never giving up
Which one will be vanished?

Just keep breathing
Keep my heart pumping
That's how I can survive

Will they ever be one again?
Maybe when my demons are defeated
Maybe then...

In my dreams

A bittersweet mirage
Tempting my tortured heart
My thoughts are swirling in circles
I don't know what's the end or the start

Shadows of what was
And what could have been
Still staring blindly
Trying to uncover the unseen

Whispers of the past
Are drawing me in
Tangles of your love
Touching my ice cold skin

Cravings, too hard to neglect
Sleeping to survive
Just want to close my eyes
Because in my dreams you are still alive...

Cravings, too hard to neglect
Sleeping to survive
Just want to close my eyes
Because in my dreams you are still alive...

Wake up!

Fear is rushing through my body
My heart is freezing of despair
Cold shivers down my spine
Trying to wake up, desperately

This has to stop, I can't take it
Breathing fast and shallow
Trying to keep it all together
Agitation is breaking my spirit

Dark images rushing by
I have to get out of this
Can't take it much longer
My mind is switching to standby

A nightmare, so horrifying
Fear and pain so deep
I have to wake up now!
Except...

My eyes are wide open and I'm not asleep

Desert of Lost Memories

Lightning strikes
Upon this barren land
A land that once held so many promises
But has nothing now since love got banned

Black clouds
Are darkening this place
A place that once was a safe haven
Now it's just an empty, nightmarish space

Withered flowers
Covering broken dreams
A desert of lost memories
Sugarcoated with the demons' screams

Swirling rivers
Made of bitter tears
Soundless crying from a torn up soul
Heartless laughter filled with fears

Insanity rises
All has become undone
Everything seems unimportant now
Because my one, true love is gone...

〇

The Darkness inside

When it's getting late
And I am getting tired
The Darkness falls in
And rises inside of me

When the distractions are gone
My confidence disappears with them
The silence is fading in
And Chaos is rising inside of me

When I lay down my head
And slowly drift away
Doubt and losses will visit
And Fear rises inside of me

When the memories are closing in
The Terror will surround me
And I will have to fight until the break of dawn
Against the demons inside of me

When the night is falling
It's not the dark outside that scares me
But being alone with my thoughts
And the Darkness inside of me...

Missing...

I don't seem able to find my heart
There's just an empty space
A hole in my chest
My heart is vanished without a trace

Don't seem to be able to find the air to breathe
Grasping for oxygen all day long
Feeling hollow inside
I am so tired of being strong

Don't seem to be able to find my soul
Just a soulless creature I am now
I have no business being in the light
Just not now

I feel robbed, cold and alone
Black thoughts fill my mind
Hold them, for they are all that I have left
There's nothing else to find

Missing my heart, my lungs, my soul
Missing...you
Without you, I just can't be whole

Guess I was wrong

Guess I was wrong
All along
I have lost this fight

I should've never believed
Got deceived
I have lost all hope

Guess it was a mirage
Ruthless sabotage
I have lost my strength

I should've kept my mask
Impossible task
I have lost my heart

Guess it wasn't even real
Devastating steal
I have lost you

Guess it wasn't even real

Devastating steal

I have lost you...

Move forward

Walking through the Desert of Emptiness
Never seem to be able
To reach the Oases of Happiness

Climbing the Mountain of Despair
Trying to reach the sanctuary at the top
But I never seem to get there

Struggling through the Woods of Grief
Just don't seem to get out
I can't get any relief

Swimming in an Ocean of Tears
Trying so hard to get across
Defeated by my fears

Crawling through the Valley of Darkness
Will I ever make it?
To the Shelter of Brightness

I will keep moving forward
No matter what
Just never give up
I will get that fresh start!

Never alone

A crowded place
No space to breath
Haunting memories
Always lurking beneath

Screaming voices
So very loud
Ongoing madness
Don't go a day without

Visiting when I sleep
Waking me up
Flashing images
Will it ever stop?

Calm on the outside, but inside...
A swirling cyclone
Because, of my demons
I am never alone

Shadows of the past

Shadows of the past
Crawling into the present
I should've know it wouldn't last
But I thought...just for a moment...

Living inside a broken dream
Build on false promises
I am floating helplessly downstream
For once...I was too careless...

Drowning in a sea of lies
Tasting bitter as hell
Those heartbreaking goodbyes
But I...just can't say farewell...

Fighting to stay sane
Losing grip by losing another
Again, battling this pain
Searching...for an answer...

Welcome back

My old nightmares return
Creeping up behind me
So afraid to lose you
I will give up willingly

Invading darkness
Sacrificing my heart
Until there is nothing left
To break apart

Can't handle this again
I will just go and hide
Being comfortably numb
And hold on to my pride

Don't come any closer
I rather turn away
Than surrender my soul
You will leave anyway

Giving up trust
I'm running of the track
The demons inside me awake
And whisper: 'Welcome back'

Wrong Love

Poisonous love
Consuming me whole
But I can't let it go
Oh! It's tearing up my soul!

Devastating love
Making me blind
But I won't give it up
Oh! It's destroying my mind!

Addicting love
My heart continues to bleed
But I just can't stop
Oh! It's like a drug I need!

Dangerous love
Razor sharp edges are hurting
But I can't ignore it
Oh! This slowly killing!

Smothering love
I shall never be free
But I will not leave
Oh! You will destroy me!

Smothering love
I shall never be free
But I will not leave
Oh! You will destroy me!

A warrior's tears

A warrior's tears
Invisible, but there nonetheless
Tearing a heart apart
Leaving nothing but emptiness

A warrior's tears
Unknowable to most
Dark and consuming thoughts
Leaving only demons and ghosts

A warrior's tears
Only the strong will know
Breaking silently into pieces
But still keeping up the show

A warrior's tears
Not falling from an eye
But burning through a soul
With every goodbye

A warrior's tears
Yours and mine
They'll keep on flowing
Until the day we will resign

Bitter April

April...
Bitter, bitter sweet April
The beginning of a new spring
The month my nightmares will begin

April...
Bitter, bitter sweet April
I am just trying to survive
The memory of your lost life

April...
Bitter, bitter sweet April
Every year it's the same
All that's lingering in my mind is your name

April...
Bitter, bitter sweet April
I am just unable to forget
You only live inside my heart and head

April...
Bitter, bitter sweet April
Will the pain ever fade away?
Can't wait until I can sleep again
Can't wait until it's May...

Invite Darkness

Invite Darkness
My old friend
Safe for my sorrows
Swirling in Madness

Losing courage
Just lay down
Giving up the fight
Broken in advantage

Sealed inside
Keeping everything out
Be on my own
Caring is denied

Closed heart
Feelings locked away
No one gets in
I don't want to fall apart

Closed heart
Feelings locked away
No one gets in
I don't want to fall apart

Nightmares returned

Horrific Nightmares
Screaming and crying, I can't stop
Like an actress in a horror story
And I am unable to wake up

Terrifying Nightmares
You kept them away
Now they're not only darkening my nights
But also my day

Victorious Nightmares
They win this battle from me
I am hiding inside myself again
They won't let me be free

Disgusting Nightmares
No hope for recovery
I have to battle them on my own
Why did you leave me?

Endless Nightmares
Staying for eternity
Never shall I escape this dark forest
And the demons that are hunting me

Screaming inside a snowstorm

Trying to escape
This ongoing agony
It's like a repeating tape
Destroying every piece of me

Trying to run from
This endless nightmare
That hits like a bomb
And follows me everywhere

Trying to heal
These wounds carved in my soul
That make me kneel
And swallowing me whole

Trying to break free
This unbearable torture
The darkness inside of me
How much more can I endure?

Trying to get warm
These cold memories are freezing me
It's like screaming inside a snowstorm
And nobody can hear me...

Bring me back to life

Hiding blindly, deep inside
Lost, I can't break free
The will to survive pushed aside
Strength is sleeping tiredly

My wounds are far too deep
They are never able to heal
Courage is fast asleep
I am numb, I cannot feel

You touched my core
Fixed a bit of my soul
I feel better than before
Although I am still out of control

Trust is lost, truth behold
Just let me be
My dead heart is so cold
And the darkness is still holding me

Spirit is sleeping, no response
There is nothing inside to save
Maybe you can wake me with a séance
I will wait for someone who is that brave

Not Again

I have felt this way before
Can't take it anymore
Not again...
This curse

Cold to the bone
Heart turning into stone
Not again...
This agony

Devastatingly alone and sad
It's driving me mad
Not again...
This torture

Wounds, unable to heal
Losing touch with what's real
Again...
This life

The demon's bride

The demon smiles
Because of my sin
I have run a thousand miles
But I can't get away from him

Begging for forgiveness
Escape this devilish deal
Screaming until I'm breathless
And I don't know what's real

The demon comes closer
Greed blinks in his eyes
And the light grows dimmer
When he leaves his disguise

No one hears my plea
In this world of despair
And all of my sanity
Vanishes into thin air

Life is a unfair game
My last hope died
And so I became
The demon's bride

Life is a unfair game
My last hope died
And so I became
The demon's bride

My frozen heart

My delightedly frozen heart
Laying perfectly still
Dodging pain and sorrow
Defusing my iron will

My polished frozen heart
Comfortably in denial
Blind for the world
Mistakenly peaceful

My blissfully frozen heart
Resting so willingly
No wandering thoughts
Logic would disagree

My pleasantly frozen heart
Shockingly cold
Forgetting the truth
Beautiful lies to hold

My lovely frozen heart
Silently giving up the fight
Maybe it will be shocked to life again
Just not tonight...

I once thought

I actually thought, just for a moment
That I could choose who I wanted to be
Leave off my mask
Just be the real me

I really thought, just for once
That people would take me as I am
No matter what and always
That someone would give a damn!

I just thought, for a second
That I could really trust someone
Someone who would never leave me
No matter what I've done

I truly thought, just for a while
That my wounds would heal
And I could leave it all behind
I believed that my dream was real

I once thought...

But now I know better
I can't escape what life made of me
What a fool I've been!
For believing in what could never be

Take over

Can't handle this anymore
Just take over
My soul has been so sore
And my heart is broken

I will fight your battles for you
Just let me take over
Helping is all I want to do
I am always here

Can't trust anyone
Just take over
I want it to be done
Do what you've got to do

I will destroy your enemies for you
Just let me take over
Care for you is what I do
I am always here

Can't feel anything anymore
Just take over
Lock me behind a closed door
And call me when it's over

I will be your hate
Make sure you no longer care
And vanishing will be your fate
Because you let me take over...

Delirium called Life

A mind wandering through the catacombs of sanity
Deprived of all humanity
Longing for the merciful death so eagerly
Reason torn up by strife

Feelings swept away by hungry madness
Overgrown by consuming coldness
Demanding the last heartbeat so anxious
Going berserk in overdrive

A soul being drenched in unescapable death
This lifeless story been read
Hoping for that all ending last breath
Mistakenly still alive

Senses roaming through blinding emptiness
Filled with horrifying absurdness
Of a deserted life living in pitiful loneliness
A place no one can survive

A heart beating steady on the rhythm of hatred
Bloodless thoughts, sick and twisted
Painful, destructive sorrow that never ended
In this ongoing delirium called Life

PART 2

MY LIGHT WINGS

But you...

The sun
Is warming my face
But your touch
Is warming my heart

The water
Is cleansing my body
But your smile
Is cleansing my soul

The wind
Is soothing my skin
But your eyes
Are soothing my spirit

The moon
Is guarding my path
But your love
Is guarding my heart

Nature
Is making me enjoy this day
But you...
Are making me enjoy life

Nature
Is making me enjoy this day
But you...
Are making me enjoy life

I shall be your guardian

I shall protect you
Against any danger
With all that I am
Be still

I shall defend you
Against any evil
With all of my power
Be still

I shall fight for you
Against any enemy
With all of my courage
Be still

I shall shield you
From any harm
With my life
So be still

For I shall be your guardian
And you are safe with me

A Thousand kisses

A thousand kisses
Some soft, like butterflies
Barely touching the skin
So sweet and gentle
Make you tremble deep within

A thousand kisses
Some hot, like fire
Sending your emotions down the highway
Glowing and burning
Let you slowly melt away

A thousand kisses
Some filled with promises
Others dazzling with regrets
A thousand meanings
Singing a thousand duets

A thousand kisses
Telling you what words can't
Expressing feelings so deep
Your lips can only pass them
Without the restriction of words to keep

A thousand kisses
On a thousand places
Each of them of the greatest value
Because a kiss is still the best way to say
'I love you'

Enjoy!

Enjoy every moment of every day
Take your time to go out and play

Enjoy the times when all goes well
And when it's bad, do not dwell

Enjoy every beat your heart is willing to give
Make it count, for as long as you live

Enjoy the things you like, endure the things you do not
Count your blessings, there are a lot

Enjoy the love of the people surrounding you
Pick yourself up when you're feeling blue

Enjoy every smile, every splinter of fun
Enjoy your life, you will only get one...

Lean on me

Captivated in your own mind
Guarded by your sorrow
Searching for happiness to find
But everything seems so hollow

All of your thoughts are black
A prison build by your past
Can't find your way back
You think good times will never last

Endless pain and suffering
Have broken your wings
But don't you stop fighting
You never know what the future brings

Once, I was frozen and dark too
Just know that someday you will be free
And I will do anything to save you
Always, you can lean on me

Path of life

Everyone has a path in life, people say
Some are rough, some made of stone
Maybe mine will be revealed as well some day
But I rather make my own

Sometimes there will be difficulties on your way
They can hold you back a bit
Just take them head on, I say
And deal with them as you see fit

There will be obstacles on your path
They say it's not smart to push through
'You'll have to go around' people say sad
But that's something I won't do!

Maybe I will get lost on the way
I don't mind, just wandering around is nice too
If I'm unable to stay on my path, I will stray
And I'll find my way back, I always do

I will get there eventually
Because I won't quit until my journey is done
Keep on going until I am where I want to be
And if I lose my way, I'll just create a new one!

I will get there eventually
Because I won't quit until my journey is done
Keep on going until I am where I want to be
And if I lose my way, I'll just create a new one!

Love...

A feeling so soft, yet so strong
Can feel so right and so wrong
It can pick you up or bring you down
Makes you smile, makes you frown

Can last forever or for a day
Makes you want to run, makes you want to stay
Grows slowly or in a second
Makes you better or gets you poisoned

Makes you happy or lose your mind
Can make you see or make you blind
Comes in so many shapes and sizes
Two of a kind or different races

Love...
Has so many unseen effects
Can be so difficult and complex
But, even when it's whispered
Love stays such a simple word
It just can't be misread...

I shall be me

I won't bow my head
Not for anyone
Never shall I beg for help
I can fight my battles on my own

I will never give up
Not for anything
Never shall I quit
I will just keep going

I shall not be imprisoned
Not by anyone
Never shall I surrender
I will fight to be free

I won't lose my pride
Not for anything
Never shall I lose myself
To please someone

I shall hold my head up high
Straighten my back
Look life right in the eye
I shall be me!

A wish

A falling star crosses the dark sky
I make a wish with closed eyes
Not for fame or fortune
Neither to become old and wise

The falling star slowly fades away
But I am still wishing
Not for health or a long life
Neither for a vacation in spring

Upon this falling star
I am wishing with all of my heart
Not for kindness or beauty
No, I don't want anything for me...

If this falling star is real
Then I am wishing for you
To become happy one day
And that your dreams may come true...

At least I am still me

I may do before I think
Listen to my feelings instead of my brain
My actions are not logical for everyone
Sometimes even a little insane...

I may act by the heart
Believe and get smacked down
My courage overflows my carefulness
Maybe that will make some frown

I may cross oceans for someone who would let me drown
I may get betrayed time after time
But that's just who I am
And at least my choices are mine

Carved into my soul

You
Inscribed into my life

Your voice
Burned into my memory

Your words
Sealed into my mind

You
Merged into my being

Your eyes
Forged into my thoughts

Your love
Engraved into my heart

You
Carved into my soul

For the rest of my life

You...

Your eyes
Forged into my thoughts

Your love
Engraved into my heart

You...
Carved into my soul

Just Patty

Dreams

Some are big
Others just small
And you'll have to choose
Can't have them all

Some come true
Others can not
A few you remember
But most you forgot

Some are important
Others, you can live without
For some you'll have to fight
But others are on your route

Some last a day
Others a lifetime
Dreaming at night
But also at daytime

Dreams...
Some are possible
Others are not
But you'll have to dream on
Sometimes it's all that you got

I love you

I love you
Just three words, easy to say
But if they're spoken from the heart
You have a friend from whom you never part

I love you
If someone means it
For some, words that are easily shared
They can make cheeks turn red

I love you
Not always true
Just meant by a handful of friends
They will stay until it all ends

I love you
Those three little words
Sometimes escape my lips
Although it makes me vulnerable
It just sometimes slips

I love you
It can't be denied
Sincerely and forever
If I say it out loud
I won't leave you, ever

I love you
Don't speak them too soon
Only say it when you are certain
Before an innocent heart
Might get broken...

I will stay wild

You can never tame me
I will stay wild
And if you try, I will break free

I don't walk the line
That's not my style
But if I have my freedom, I'll be fine

Don't you chain me, that's not right
I can't be caged
I will just fight!

Please, don't try to break me
It won't work, I won't bow
You shall never possess me

Never tell me what to do
I won't listen, make you mad
And then I will just smile at you

So if you really love me
Don't bind my wings
And I will stay with you
Maybe...

Choose

Instead of breaking
I will keep fighting

Instead of crying
I will be laughing

Instead of giving up
I will struggle through

Instead of despair
I will have hope

Instead of hate
I will feel love

That's the way I choose to live my life
And that's the way I will survive

My child

Whatever you may do
Whoever you may become
I will always love you

Wherever you may go
Wherever you have been
I will follow

I will fight for you
Until my very last breath
I will help you through

I will comfort you, hold you close
Scare away your fears
Wipe all of your tears
Protect you against your foes

Because, my child, can't you see?
You are the best part of me there will ever be...

Relax

Relax...
Take your time
Don't stress out
Chill, before you get a burn-out

Relax...
Take your rest
Even when you're busy
Life is too precious to be hasty

Relax...
Just stay calm
Don't run all day
You will run your life away

Relax...
Don't worry so much
Have some fun
A smile is worth a billion

Relax...
I will promise you
The world will survive
Even if you take five...

Can't resist

One smile from you
And I can feel the sparkle
It just makes my day
When you are playful

One look in your eyes
And my body starts to tremble
I am longing for your touch
It's almost painful

One touch of you
And I will start to dazzle
I am going to lose my mind
That's clear as crystal

One kiss from you
Is almost more than I can handle
The feelings that are taking over
Are so darn powerful!

And when I am alone with you...
Oh, I know I'm in trouble
There's no way I can resist
I am just not able

And when I am alone with you...
Oh, I know I'm in trouble
There's no way I can resist

I am just
not
able

Touched your heart

Every once in a while
Someone touches your heart
And you will love this person
Right from the start

Your trust and smiles
Others had to gain
You'll give this person freely
It's like a malfunction of the brain

Someone touched your heart
So you can't help it
You will give yourself over
Bit by bit...

A connection so strong, it can't be broken
Not by distance, not by time
With some people
You will always have that line

People give that connection a name
Call it chemistry, call it love
Call it an act from the heavens above...

Fact is, it can't be explained
Why between some, that feeling is real
Someone just touched your heart...
At least, that's how I feel

As long as...

Give me your fears
I will send you courage

Give me your nightmares
I will turn them into dreams

Give me your tears
I will make you smile

Give me your anger
I will show you love

Give me your desperation
I will give you hope instead

Give me what's broken
I will fix it for you

I will do it all
As long as I can keep you...

Love & Hate

Love is a four letter word
So is Hate...
They both spring from passion
And they're both very strong

Hate can keep you going
So can Love...
They both can rule your life
And they both can break you

Love can fill your heart
So can Hate...
They both promise satisfaction
And they both can drive you insane

Hate and Love
They are much alike
But Love can bring Life
And Hate can only take it away...

My Knight

I was wandering on a battlefield when he found me
Wounded by life, about to surrender
Surrounded by demons who were screaming devilishly

Like a ball of pure light he came and held me close
Confused me with his kindness
I couldn't believe it was me he chose

He pulled me up and refused to let go
Breathing life into my barren soul
Awakened my heart, more than he will ever know

He looked inside me and decided to stay
Gave me love and kept me safe
Scared my most devastating demons away

All these years, he fought by my side
Got wounded bad, but never backed down
Saving my life countless times, never did he hide

A warrior, made of pure light and love
My knight, who keeps me alive
A savior, sent from the heavens above

Maybe his armor is not that shiny anymore
We have been through a lot
But his beautiful soul shines as never before

With this strong, handsome knight in my life
Who I love with all of my heart
There is nothing I can't survive

Not your decision

You can push me away
Try to convince me that you are gone
But I will just stay...
Because I knew all along

You can hurt me, pretend to be heartless
Trying to say goodbye
But I just couldn't care less...
Because love like ours doesn't die

You can turn your back on me
Trying to get me to hate you
But our connection is supposed to be...
And I know it will stay true

You can pretend it was all fake
Just do what you want to do
Because it's not your decision...
If whether or not I will love you

You can hurt me,
pretend to be heartless

Trying to say goodbye

But I just couldn't care less...

Because love like ours doesn't die

Just Patty

The girl in the picture

Can't you see?
That little girl in the picture
That little girl is me!

Oh, my life was so easy and kind
Filled with joy and laughter
Every day new adventures to find

Promises, big and small
Fairytales all around
And I believed in them all

But somewhere along the way
Things changed and I learned
That not all is meant to stay

I became wiser, grew up
Lost faith, broke down, fought back
Changed my clothes, tried on make-up

Seems like only yesterday...
That this little girl trusted the whole wide world
At the same time, it seems like a thousand nightmares away

My heart got broken, a waterfall of tears
Disappointed and betrayed
But also a lot of fun throughout the years!

Now, my life has changed a lot
Many years have gone by
My dreams from the past...I forgot

But...can't you see?
Somewhere, deep inside
That little girl in the picture
That girl is still me!

My precious dreamer

I love my fellow dreamer
The one that dreams along with me
About the future...
How things could be

Together, we reshape the world
Make it exactly how we want it to be
It's really amazing...
You should see!

Sharing dreams creates a bond
Strong and carefree
And maybe someday...
Our dreams will become reality

So keep dreaming with me, my precious dreamer
It will keep us young of heart
Through our dreams we stay connected
And it helps us when life gets hard...

Never giving up

Never
Shall I give up
I will hang on
And I will not stop

Always
Staying strong
I will not break
When things go wrong

Never
Letting go
I shall not bow
For things that are lurking in the shadow

Always
Having hope
Believe it will be alright
Holding on to the last rope

Never
Shall I turn my back
I will be here
Even when you turn black

Always
Pushing through
I will stay on your side
Never...
Shall I give up on you

Song of my heart

A melody
Plays inside my mind
Resonating every fiber of me
The sweetest notes combined

A rhythm
Vivacious rushing through my veins
All obstacles can be overcome
The beauty is what remains

A dance
Swirling through my soul
Delightedly lost in trance
The music is in control

A song
Created by my heart
Listen to it all night long
The most enchanting art

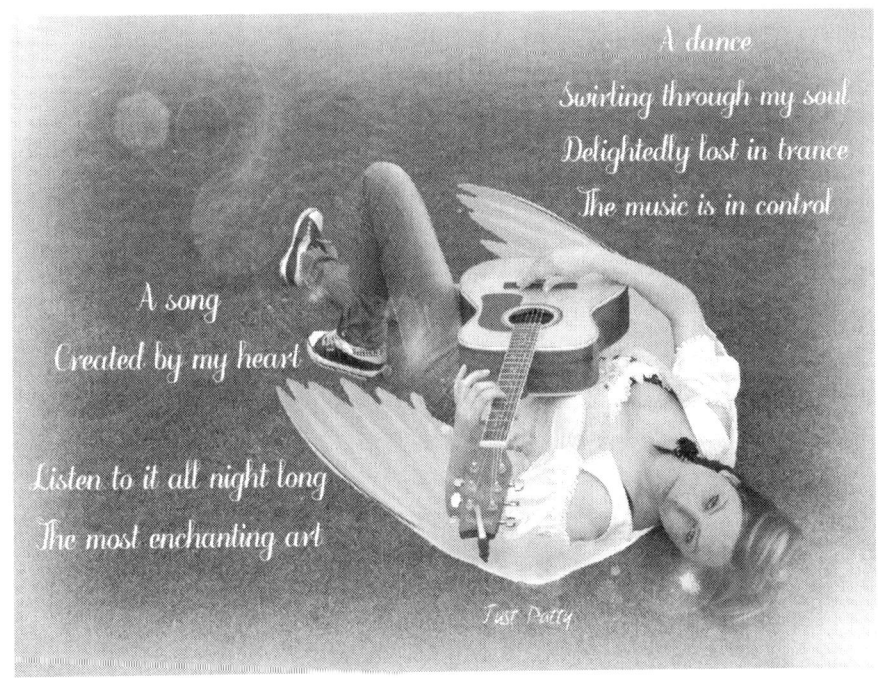

A dance
Swirling through my soul
Delightedly lost in trance
The music is in control

A song
Created by my heart

Listen to it all night long
The most enchanting art

Just Pretty

The roads untraveled

What would have happened
If I would've gone left instead of right?
Traveling in a different direction...
Would the future have been more bright?

What would have been different?
If I would've chosen other options
Would it have been more easy...
If I had taken other actions?

What would it have been like
If I would've walked another path?
Would it all have been better...
Or would it only have brought regret?

All of the choices we make
Would it someday all be unraveled?
Maybe in the end we will be able to see...
The roads untraveled

Finally

You have built up hope
But all you know is failure
Remembering all the pain and frustration
Until it's just a blur

You try again, over and over
But it never seems to work out
Fading into darkness
Again drowning in doubt

You will have to fight for what you want
But it's so damn hard
Life just doesn't seem to give you a break
And you pull up your guard

You can't give up
Some day you will win
Fall down 7 times, stand up 8
And your life can finally begin!

Love me for who I am

Love me for who I am
Or don't love me at all
Because for fake friends
My world is just too small

Love me for who I am
Or just let me be
I don't want your attention
Unless it's given freely

Love me for who I am
With my buckets of crazy
But if you're not brave enough
Just walk away cowardly

If you really love me
You will love the way I am
Damaged, stubborn, loyal and free
So, try to love me, if you dare
Love me for who I am!

Once upon a time...

Locked up in a tower of despair
Unable to find the key
In another world I would braid my hair
So you could climb up and rescue me

Caught in a devastating nightmare
There's no way to let it stop
I wished I lived elsewhere
So you could kiss me and wake me up

The beast keeps me against my will
I have nowhere to run
But in that world that isn't real
You would slay that fiery dragon

In that fairytale land, far far away
You can be my knight in shining armor
Everything would be okay
And we would live happily ever after...

Dear Life

If you want me to bow
I will stand up straight
You can kick me down today
But I will stand up tomorrow

If you want me to cry
I will gladly smile
I will laugh every day
Until the day I die

If you want me to hate
I will share the love
Depending on my own free will
And not just fate

If you want me to give up
I will struggle through
Continue fighting my battles
And I will never stop

If you want me to walk away
I will be going nowhere
You can push me over the edge
I will just find another way

If you want to break me
I will stay strong
Because I will be able
To still see the beauty

So dear Life, can't you see?
I am still a warrior
And there is no way
You can ever defeat me!

You

You
Scratched your name
Across my heart
So deep and sudden
Irreversible

And now
Even when you leave
Or don't love me anymore

The scar
Will stay there
Across my heart
Forever

You
Scratched your name
Across my heart
So deep and sudden
Irreversible

Friends

There are friends you will have forever
And friends you'll have just for a while
Friends that make you cry
And friends that make you smile

There are friends who are there for you
And friends who are not
Friends you will remember
And friends you forgot

There are friends who are always loyal
And friends who betray
Friends who are local
And friends who live far away

There are friends who will stay in your life
And friends just for a season
Friends come and go
But you always meet a friend for a reason...

Every time

Every time I look into your eyes
I feel my love for you grow
Just like the first time I fantasized
That we belonged together

Every time you grab my hand
I feel blessed and safe
Right by your side I stand
For the rest of our lives

Every time you hold me close
I feel sheltered against the world
You are the one I chose
We are made for each other

Every time you kiss me
I feel the passion deep within
And if loving you would be forbidden
I would gladly live in sin...

Just be you

You don't have to write me a song
Or buy me a diamond ring
I don't care if you're strong
Or just a scrawny little thing

You don't have to be my hero
I can save myself, don't worry
Don't care if you are macho or mellow
Or if you are just crazy

You don't have to drive a nice car
Or solve my problems for me
I like you just the way you are
And I like your company

You don't have to be popular
Or have a lot of money
I don't care if you're ugly or pretty
I just really don't care

So, just make me smile and be true
Be my friend and care for me
You are just fine, being you
That's all I want you to be

Smile again

Always keep your head up
Never let life get you down
Be brave, be strong
Even if everything goes wrong
Someday you will smile again...

Always remember the good things
Don't focus on the bad
Be fierce, be hopeful
Even if everything seems awful
Someday you will smile again...

Always keep going
Never break
Be optimistic, be faithful
Even if it's a daily battle
Someday you will smile again...

In the meantime
I will be here for you
Fighting with you, holding you close
Encourage you on the path you chose
Hoping to see you smile again...

I have you

When my world gets covered by darkness
At least I'll still have you
All that I need to survive
Is your freely given kindness

When everything goes to waste
It's alright as long as I have you
To remind me forever
How good life can taste

When I seem lost for a moment
I know it's okay
Because I'll have you next to me
To make the world a bit more pleasant

When I lose my courage
And I get judged by the crowd
I know I can lean on you
And I will heal from any damage

When things go bad
And I can't get up
I know you will stay with me
The sweetest love I ever had

When things go bad
And I can't get up
I know you will stay with me
The sweetest love I ever had

I am here for you

I know that you are hurting now
Please, don't bleed out
I will heal you

I know that you are crying now
Please, don't drown
I will dry your tears

I know that you are hanging on the edge now
Please, don't let go
I will catch you

I know that you are lost right now
Please, don't disappear
I will find you

I know that you feel defeated now
Please, don't give up
I will fight for you

And even if you are broken now
Please, don't fall apart
I will fix you

If you just let me...

Out of the shadows

Waiting for my moment
My chance
To escape this judgment
And take control of my life

Waiting for tomorrow
A better day
Today will never come back though
An endless waiting for next time

Waiting for a miracle
To be happy
When will I finally be able
To live the life I want?

Waiting in the shadows for my time to come
Searching for a way
Out of the slavery my life has become
Out of the night, into the day

But now I can see
And I am done waiting
I shall make my own destiny
And live the life I've been craving

If I could, I would

If I could, I would take it all away
Your pain, your sorrow
Turn your night into day
I would be your hero

If I could, I would carry all of your burdens
Your struggles, your fear
Move the mountains
Until your sky is clear

If I could, I would fight all of your battles
Your past, your future
Surround you with guardian angels
Make your life brighter

If I could, there is nothing I wouldn't do
I would commit any crime
But I can only promise you
To love you until the end of time...

If I could, there is nothing I wouldn't do
I would commit any crime
But I can only promise you
To love you until the end of time...

No genie

Changes
Don't come easy
You will have to fight
To become happy

Strength
Is needed
You can't give up
Until you've succeeded

Hope
For a better future
Leaving the past behind
And heal from the torture

Believe
That you can make it
This time for real
Step by step, bit by bit

Courage
To push through
There's no genie in a bottle
It's all up to you

Proud to be me

For the ones I love, I am a blessing
But I'm a living nightmare for those I hate
I am a crazy and chaotic little thing
And I make my own fate

I can be smart and tremendously stupid
I am courageous and loyal
There's no box I actually fit
And if I love, I will give it my all

I can drive someone crazy
Can be dark and I am light
My spirit is always free
And I don't back down from a fight

I either care too much or not at all
Get myself into trouble, sometimes willingly
But I am strong and I stand tall
And I am proud to be me!

What I want to do

Keeping you safe forever
Is what I want to do
Be your armor
To protect you

Making you laugh until you cry
Is what I want to do
Be a sun in a cloudless sky
Every day anew

Always holding you tight
Is what I want to do
Be your shelter, day and night
Always comforting you

Let you be the one you want to be
Is what I want to do
Because who you really are
Is just perfect for me

Will you?

If I leave
Will you follow?

If I am fighting
Will you protect me?

If I am lost
Will you find me?

If I fall
Will you catch me?

If I whisper
Will you hear me?

If I seek shelter
Will you hide me?

If I am broken
Will you fix me?

And if I care for you...
Will you let me?

That light in my life

Through the darkest of days
It always shines upon me
Shows me a way out of this maze
This web of misery

Through black clouds and heavy storm
It will always find me
A light so gentle and warm
Treasured and lovely

Through times of hell
It's always there for me
To make sure that I do not dwell
Or spend my days in agony

A light of healing
Helping me to survive
And I thank you for being
That light in my life

A light of healing
Helping me to survive
And I thank you for being
That light in my life

If you...

If you care, tell me
If you love me, show me
I won't believe you right away
But don't give up, just stay

My trust is not easy to gain
It takes a lot of effort
I am a bit insecure
And will always be alert

But...

If you think of me, let me know
If you like me, say that also
I may keep you away for a while
But don't go, just smile

My love is not given easily
But it's always true
Only when I am certain
I will say: I love you

So...

If you are real, prove it
If you love me, say it
I may believe you eventually
And give you the love that's built up inside of me

Keep smiling

Keep smiling, just keep smiling
No matter how hard life is some days
Lift your head up and stay strong
Remember the good moments always

Keep smiling, just keep smiling
Endure the pain with grace
Never give up and laugh at sorrow
There are a lot of moments to embrace

Keep smiling, just keep smiling
Enjoy life to the full
Share love as much as you can
There's always a way to be grateful

Keep smiling, just keep smiling
Have fun until the end
That's the way we choose to live
That's how we create our moments, my friend

No matter what

No matter what
Don't give up
Fight for a better day
And never stop

No matter how dark
There will be light
Just have to believe
That it's going to be alright

No matter the struggles
You'll have to go through
As long as your heart beats
There's always hope for you

No matter how hard
Life is going to be
Stay brave and strong
Let your soul be free

No matter the cost
Keep the faith alive
That's the way
You can survive

No matter the cost
Keep the faith alive
That's the way
You can survive

Fun?

Fun?
Anyone?
Or busy as usual...
Don't have time for anything at all

Fun?
Anyone?
Just take the day off
To spend with the people you love

Fun?
Anyone?
Try to have some every day
It will blow your sorrows away!

Fun?
Anyone?
It won't take a lot of your time
Having fun is not a crime

Fun?
Anyone?
Running, cleaning, working
Boring, boring, boring...

Fun?
Anyone?

ANYONE???

My sister's keeper

My sister's keeper, I'll always be
Even though she's older than me
Our bond is strong and will never break
Always looking out for each other's sake

I am my sister's keeper
With my life I will defend her
Share our laughs and sometimes a tear
Remember sis, I'm always here

I'm my sister's keeper and she is mine
Whatever may happen in time
No one can ever come between us
It is a honor to call her 'Zus'

Between friends, love can be strong
It can even last a lifetime long
Between sisters, that feeling is even deeper
I am, and always will be, my sister's keeper

An Angel

I have found an angel
Fallen from heaven
Someone so gentle
And as bright as the sun

Wings of unbelievable softness
Not from this earth
Heart of unspeakable kindness
Which I don't believe to be worth

Did this angel really fall for me?
Someone this pure and kind
But also wild and free
With blue eyes that make me lose my mind

I am just a mortal soul
Nothing special really
Sometimes even out of control
So, why should I be so lucky?

But still, this lovely angel
Is spending his life with me
And I am eternally grateful
To have found a love so heavenly

Never leave you alone

I just could not trust
Anyone anymore
Too many times I bite the dust
Just afraid to let you in

Maybe I was wrong
Holding back
Because I loved you all along
And you are a part of me

But I am telling you now
Never walk out
I shall not break, I shall not bow
Never leave you alone

I will catch you if you fall
Hold you close
We will fight and beat it all
Never losing hope

Leap of faith

Don't try to fix me
Even though I might be broken
I may be in pieces
But I haven't become undone

Don't try to erase me
And draw me anew
I may not be what you want
But I don't need a rescue

Don't try to cage me
Even though I might be wild
I will fight you
And I won't be mild

Don't try to change me
Because it won't last
I am who I am today
Because of my past

I will take a leap of faith
And show you who I am truly
But don't try to make me into something I am not
Just accept me being me...

I will take a leap of faith
And show you who I am truly
But don't try to make me into something I am not
Just accept me being me...

I won't give up on us

Life has a habit of driving us mad
Nothing ever comes easy
Times we are angry, times we are sad
Times that we live in agony

This war we'll fight together, not alone
Nothing is gained without a battle
Times we have peace, times we will find our own
Times we have to struggle

We might fall, but we will learn
Nothing comes by itself
Times we are happy, times we earn
Just have to believe in yourself

Someday we will have the life we want
Nothing can hold us back
Times we'll have fun, remember our bond
Just have to stay on track

We will stick together, no matter what
Just take my hand
One time we'll be victorious, nothing can tear us apart
You are my friend until the end

I won't give up on us...

Special Thanks

I want to thank my cousin Sheryl for helping me with some of the photos that led to the artwork in this book. I love you so much.

And I want to give a huge 'Thank you' to Chris and Phil, who helped me with the editing of this book. Thank you both so much for helping me to make this book as flawless as possible and helping me to understand the English language so much better. I owe you both!

I also would like to thank my family and friends for their encouragement and everlasting love that makes it possible for me to do what I love the most.

A million thanks to my friends in the blogging world who have been so supportive to me this entire journey.

Thank you all so very much.

Lots of love & Hugz

Just Patty

About the author

Just Patty is the poet name used by the Dutch writer
Patty van Delft.

Why the name 'Just Patty'?
Because writing poetry is a naked reflection of the heart and soul,
nothing more and nothing less.
It's *just you* without decorations.

The poetry by Just Patty is mostly a combination of dark thoughts,
loss, grief, love and the courage to continue fighting no matter what.

The art that Just Patty uses to illustrate her poetry is made by her.
She models for her own photos, shoots them and does the editing as
well.

*'Poetry is a way of showing your darkest thoughts and deepest feelings
through the art of words.
Listen to the music of your soul and let your pen dance to the
rhythm.'*

*Lots of Love,
Just Patty*

Printed in Great Britain
by Amazon